Steam Memories on Shed: 1950's – 1960's

No. 60: GLASGOW ENGINE SHEDS

David Dunn

Copyright Book Law Publications 2013
ISBN 978-1-907094-76-7

INTRODUCTION

Having looked at the engine sheds on the north bank of the Clyde (and beyond) in Volume 1, we now concentrate on the two big sheds on the south bank of that famous industrious waterway. It was intended to present the sheds in their two obvious groups; those under 66 district and, in a further volume, those under 67 district. However, like all well laid plans, along came a bunch of outstanding illustrations which could not be ignored or left out. So, ever open to suggestions of a positive nature, the compiler chose to concentrate on the two main depots and cover the 'garage sheds' in a subsequent album. So, here we present 66A and 67A in all their British Railways steam period glory.

Polmadie was a big shed dealing in the main with big locomotives and hopefully the illustrations herein will reflect those long gone images of 'Duchesses' 'Clans' 'Brits' 'Scots' and the myriad of other types which called Polmadie home during the period under review. Although we did not manage to illustrate the whole class – *An album of the Duchesses* was not the remit – a parade of Pacifics is on offer instead. Well what did you expect?

Corkerhill, though somewhat smaller than its former Caledonian neighbour, nevertheless held together an allocation which, though also cosmopolitan (housing three generations of standardisation), did not quite have the same magnetic draw of 66A. Nevertheless, the illustrations convey nicely the motive power depot scene during the British Railways era on the south side of Glasgow.

David Dunn, Cramlington, 2013.

Cover Picture: What better locomotive type could illustrate the front cover of an album featuring Polmadie engine shed other than a Semi', or 'Princess Coronation', or a 'Duchess'. Whatever title was given to these magnificent engines, it all meant the same – perfection! This is No.46225 DUCHESS OF GLOUCESTER in semi-streamlined condition outside Polmadie shed at an unknown date in the early Fifties'. The Crewe North Pacific is waiting to leave the shed and back down to Central station. *K.H.Cockerill.*

Previous Page: Three generations of motive power. Heading the queue in 1962 was ex-works and former Caley 3F 0-6-0 No.57581 looking rather magnificent after what was probably its last major overhaul. To the right is another Polmadie resident in the shape of WD 2-8-0 No.90596 which, curiously for this much maligned class, is fairly clean. On the other side of the 8F is a representative of the new generation which was about to change the face of British Railways locomotion, in the shape of English Electric Type 4 diesel-electric D331. A question often asked but as yet unanswered 'Why did Polmadie not have any of the EE Type 4s allocated, ever?' *I.W.Coulson.*

Printed and bound by The Amadeus Press, Cleckheaton, West Yorkshire
First published in the United Kingdom by Book Law Publications, 382 Carlton Hill, Nottingham, NG4 1JA

POLMADIE

A Wednesday afternoon view of Polmadie shed, or at least nine of its fourteen-road width, on 19th August 1959. Steam was still supreme and the 2-6-4Ts (42275, 42276, 80022, 80027, 80054, and 80056 are identified) are all waiting to take up duties for the evening rush. This depot had always maintained a sizeable allocation of passenger tanks for working the formidable local passenger services which not only covered the Greater Glasgow area but also services out to the west as far as the coast. At this time Polmadie could boast some forty-three 2-6-4Ts (nearly a quarter of its 180 plus total locomotive fleet), which were drawn equally from the ex-LMS and BR Standard versions; that number being up on the 1948 total of thirty-six from an overall total of just 160! By the end of the winter timetable in 1965, the 2-6-4T population at 66A had dropped to just twenty-one engines but the overall steam allocation was by then down to just forty. *David J.Dippie.*

Our first Stanier Pacific illustration reveals No.46245 CITY OF LONDON in the back yard where seven of the shed roads continued up to the embankment formed by Polmadie Road. The date is Wednesday of 19th August 1959, and the Camden based 'Duchess' is having some internal work carried out. Such work was everyday for the Polmadie fitters, their own fleet of Stanier Pacifics having taught them all there was to know about the mechanics of these superb locomotives. *David J.Dippie.*

On that very day and just to the left of the Camden engine were two of Polmadie's own: No.46230 DUCHESS OF BUCCLEUCH, the photographer's subject, and No.46222 QUEEN MARY of which only half of the front end is shown but reveals a fitter dealing with a blastpipe problem. It is notable that all three locomotives are facing the same way i.e. ready to reverse down to Glasgow (Central) station when put back into traffic but also, the natural daylight is being used to assist the work; much better than working inside the shed or the repair shop. Note that No.46245 has been fitted with ATC whereas No.46230 has yet to acquire that equipment. We shall visit this area later to look at another completely different trio of Pacifics. *David J.Dippie.*

Rebuilt 'Royal Scot' No.46105 CAMERON HIGHLANDER, in the lined black livery, which was still prevalent for some years after Nationalisation. The date of this illustration is 27th October 1951, four months after the Polmadie 'Scot' was fitted with a proper front numberplate containing Gill sans figures; the previous effort, though correctly numbered, was a mixture of the old LMS numbers and a hybrid '4'. Considering the 4-6-0 had received a Heavy Intermediate overhaul during the previous May, no effort was made to change the **BRITISH RAILWAYS** insignia on the tender for a BR emblem. That change eventually took place a full twelve months after this scene was recorded during a Heavy General overhaul when smoke deflectors were also fitted. It would be interesting to know what No.46105 had been working prior to coming on shed with a brake van. *C.J.B.Sanderson.*

The harbinger of things to come! Peppercorn A1 No.60161 NORTH BRITISH was allocated to Polmadie shed from 14th January to 11th March 1951, and then again, but for a much longer period, from 16th September 1951 to 29th June 1953! Sister No.60160 AULD REEKIE (I wonder how the Glaswegians handled that?) did a similar stint but on a different set of dates from 14th January to 4th March 1951, and 16th April 1951 to 22nd February 1952. No.60152 HOLYROOD was also involved and followed No.60161's shed movements closely at first but did not return to Polmadie for a second stint until the end of December 1952 after which it too resided until the end of the following June. So, a nice little trio of ECML Pacifics plying the WCML but add also No.60159 BONNIE DUNDEE, which was loaned to 66A for a couple of weeks in June 1951 whilst No.60160 was in works at Cowlairs. The duties carried out by the A1s consisted mainly working the 6.25 p.m. Up *POSTAL* as far as Crewe, returning with the 12.50 p.m. Birmingham-Glasgow express the following day, also the 9.25 p.m. Glasgow (Central)-London (Euston) sleeper as far as Carlisle, from where it worked back with the 3.34 a.m. Glasgow sleeper. They were apparently liked. Why the A1s were allocated to Polmadie for so long is unknown but the why can be easily deduced from the regular traffic patterns worked. So why did the ECML not entertain a Stanier Pacific on a similar basis? No.60161 is turned and coaled at Polmadie on 27th October 1951, during its second, longer stint at the shed. *C.J.B.Sanderson.*

Let's get down to business. Long time Polmadie stalwart No.46232 DUCHESS OF MONTROSE is suitably cleaned, and burnished, prior to going off shed to take on the Up working of *THE ROYAL SCOT* on Monday morning 26th May 1952. The tender springs are almost horizontal, the near twenty-nine ton payload of coal and water would lighten only gradually, at first. *C.J.B.Sanderson.*

(*above*) Crewe North's 'Princess Royal' No.46209 PRINCESS BEATRICE near the ash pits on Monday 26th May 1952. (*below*) The other side of 'Princess Coronation' No.46232 DUCHESS OF MONTROSE, on the departure road, same day. Apart from visual references, what's the difference between the two? Fifteen hundredweight according to the Ian Allan ABC! Although the 'Duchess' class always had a significant presence at Polmadie, the 'Princess Royals' were not so prolific, at least in allocation terms. Apart from four locomotives having short periods there in the 1930s: 6201 – 1/34 to 8/35; 6203 – 8/35 to 2/36; 6204 – 12/35; 6205 – 9/35 and 12/39; and four more in the 1950 and 60s: 46200 – 9/51 to 5/53; 46201 – 7/58 to 3/61; 46203 – 9/51 to 5/53; 46210 – 7/58 to 3/61; they remained fairly elusive and even skipped the 1940s completely. Note that the BR period allocations were undertaken in pairs. Our subject above was never on the books at 66A. *Both C.J.B.Sanderson.*

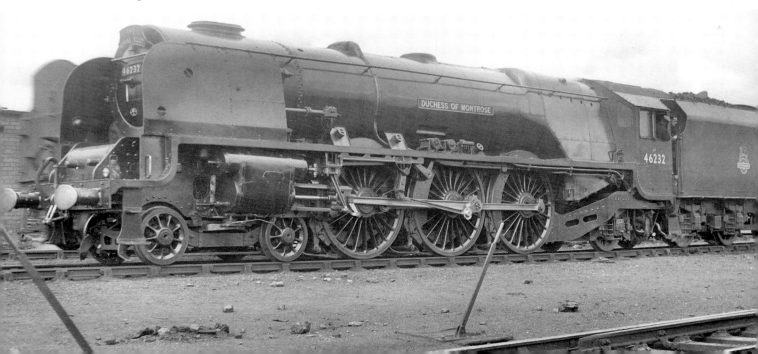

Having started our little parade of Stanier Pacifics (it is Polmadie so what did you expect), we back peddle to the beginning of the 'Princess Coronation' class and feature the engine which started it all – No.46220 CORONATION. The date is Saturday 25th October 1958 and the big green lady is having her tender topped up prior to moving off to Central station; the coal bunker is certainly full. By now the class doyen – or would doyenne be more appropriate – was a Crewe North engine having transferred away from Polmadie during the previous July, after nineteen years at Polmadie. A cleaning of sorts has been carried out but it appears that a group of Pygmies have been employed! Still times were hard for BR and any cleaning was better than none (*see later*). *C.J.B.Sanderson.*

Job done! Resident No.46221 **QUEEN ELIZABETH** takes to the turntable at the far end of the shed yard having brought the Down *ROYAL SCOT* from Carlisle for the concluding leg of its journey. After turning, the Pacific will visit the coaling plant, then the ash pits, and finally back onto one of the shed roads for a looking over and any necessary adjustments. The date is Monday 18th May 1953 and reminders of the engine's streamlined origins linger but do not detract from the stately and majestic lines. It must be said that even when they were discarded and lined up for scrap, these engines still had a presence about them which was rather grand. *C.J.B.Sanderson.*

Five years on and we find No.46222 QUEEN MARY en route to the shed after completing the servicing sequence on 25th October 1958. The new coal in the tender has yet to be trimmed and tidied-up whilst lubrication will be applied to the numerous points about the engine. A couple of hours maximum and 46222 will be ready for another outing. Of course, a diesel locomotive did not require the servicing which a steam locomotive demanded, nor did it require the huge infrastructure and capital costs nor the on-going costs of keeping that equipment working so you can see why steam was on its way out. This particular Pacific was a long-time resident of 66A and had been since December 1939 when, in the company of Nos.6223 and 6224, it was sent to Polmadie to form the backbone for the Anglo-Scottish traffic which was about to reach new wartime heights. *C.J.B.Sanderson.*

Another 'Semi', another train, another day! No.46225 DUCHESS OF GLOUCESTER makes her way off shed to power the Up, and often very heavy, working of *THE MID-DAY SCOT* on Saturday 9th May 1953. Wearing the blue lined livery of the period, the 'Duchess' was allocated to Crewe North at this time and, except for a month long loan in 1940, was never allocated to Polmadie. It was amongst the last active members of the class being withdrawn on 12th September 1964. *C.J.B.Sanderson.*

(*above*) Saturday 9th April 1955 with the yard at Polmadie filling up as locomotives finish their duties and look forward to a day of rest. Within a matter of weeks the yard would fill and stay filled for many weeks as the ASLEF strike took hold (*see also Glasgow Engine Sheds 1*). Two residents, No.46230 DUCHESS OF BUCCLEUCH and No.46227 DUCHESS OF DEVONSHIRE, settle down for the night. (*below*) A classic scene of steam, smoke, and sunshine as No.46231 DUCHESS OF ATHOLL takes on more water at Polmadie on 4th May 1957. *Both C.J.B.Sanderson.*

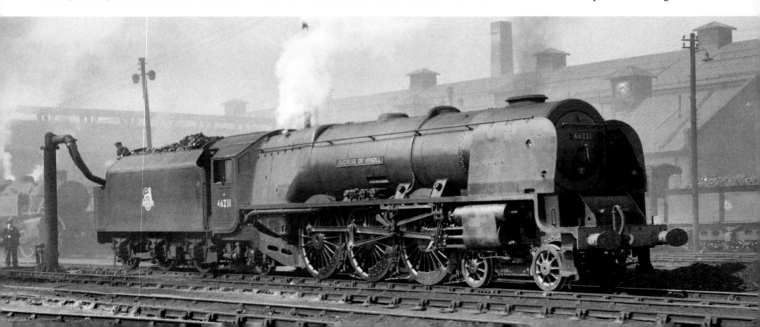

Continuing the review of ex-LMS Pacifics, we present No.46233 DUCHESS OF SUTHERLAND on 25th October 1958. A newcomer to the Crewe North allocation having transferred from Upperby during the previous September, No.46233 was sent to Edge Hill in September 1960. The final two winters of its life, 62-63 and 63-64, were spent in store and it was a week after the final one that the Pacific was condemned on 8th February 1964. *C.J.B.Sanderson.*

Destined for a cruel life in preservation, No.46235 CITY OF BIRMINGHAM is seen in happier times reversing down the yard at Polmadie en route to Central station. It is a rather dull 29th July 1957 but the big engine is behaving itself by not adding too much pollution, yet. The contents of the tender probably contravene the loading gauge by some inches – perhaps she had a reputation as a bit of a hungry lady. *C.J.B.Sanderson.*

It is late in the day for the 'Princess Coronation' class – Sunday 17th May 1964 – and No.46240 CITY OF COVENTRY is amongst the last active members of her kind, and already a 'rare' visitor to Polmadie. Less than half of the class are surviving by this time. By this date steam is banished to this, the west side of Polmadie shed (roads 1 to 7) whilst diesels have taken over the remaining seven. This engine will go out with fifteen other 'Duchesses' during the week ending 12th September, their rapid demise being something akin to indecent haste. No doubt the scrap merchants were rubbing their hands when that lot went up for tender. That left just No.46256 in traffic to work a few special duties, after which it too went for scrap. *A.Ives.*

Another livery, and another 'Duchess'. No.46248 CITY OF LEEDS takes water in 1959 from what appears to have been a favourite location for the class. A Crewe North engine at this time, this particular 'semi' was never allocated to 66A. Note that no ATC/AWS is fitted yet. Alongside is 'Royal Scot' No.46102 BLACK WATCH (*see later*). *C.J.B.Sanderson.*

No.46249 CITY OF SHEFFIELD resides at the back of the shed on Saturday 21st April 1962. No matter from which angle you view these engines, they just looked the part – bulky, powerful, able! This engine had transferred into Polmadie in March 1961 but was no stranger to Glasgow having worked through the late war years from Polmadie until moved to Upperby in October 1946. The 'Duchess' was now enjoying a final fling on the Anglo-Scottish expresses but circumstances and modernisation would catch up soon enough. Withdrawn during week ending Saturday 9th November 1963, along with shed mate 46230 DUCHESS OF BUCCLEUCH, the pair became the last of the Polmadie based Stanier Pacifics. No.46249 was not yet twenty years old but time and progress marches on relentlessly. *David J.Dippie.*

No.46250 CITY OF LICHFIELD presents a contemporary external appearance whilst waiting for release from Polmadie shed in August 1962. *David J.Dippie.*

Resting before heading south on Saturday 21st April 1962, Crewe North's No.46253 CITY OF ST ALBANS presents a reasonably clean boiler whilst the rest of the locomotive....! They were trying times. It is often forgotten that Polmadie acquired a number of ex-Midland and LMS 4F 0-6-0s to cover for withdrawn former Caledonian 0-6-0 types and one of them is just visible on the right. In 1947 Polmadie maintained exactly forty-six 0-6-0 tender engines, the majority being ex-Caley 2F and 3F examples, and amongst that number were two ex-LMS 4Fs. By the end of the 1950s the 0-6-0 tender engines allocated was down but only by one to forty-five; nothing in the way of change considering the steady loss of goods traffic during that decade. However, five of those engines were ex-LNER, a mixture from Class J35 and J36, which added further to Polmadie's 'addiction' to try anything. Besides the five mentioned, there were two others which spent time at 66A during the decade: J35 No.64464 and J36 No.65304. *David J.Dippie.*

Having run straight onto the ash pits before visiting the coaling plant, Kingmoor's No.46255 CITY OF HEREFORD has its fire cleaned on 6th August 1963. Polmadie is by now down to just five operation Stanier Pacifics with one of those imminent for withdrawal. So, the visiting engines from Carlisle and Crewe were most welcome. By the end of the year 66A will have none of these magnificent beasts on the books and in just over twelve months no other shed would either. For much of its short life this Pacific was allocated to Carlisle Upperby and had occasional forays to Camden, Crewe and even Edge Hill but Carlisle was its last home. A period of storage in early 1964 (at Upperby) would see it resurrected for its final workings in the summer of '64. At the ending of the summer timetable it was withdrawn and promptly sold for scrap. *David J.Dippie.*

The ultimate in LMS Pacific design!? With a full bunker, No.46257 CITY OF SALFORD appears ready for the road and making its way off shed on the evening of Saturday 6th May 1961. *C.J.B.Sanderson.*

Two of Polmadie's own show off their elegant lines on the shed yard on 8th May 1954. (*above*) DUCHESS OF ATHOLL, is ready for a southbound working. (*below*) DUCHESS OF MONTROSE makes her way to the starting blocks on the same afternoon. Both *C.J.B.Sanderson*.

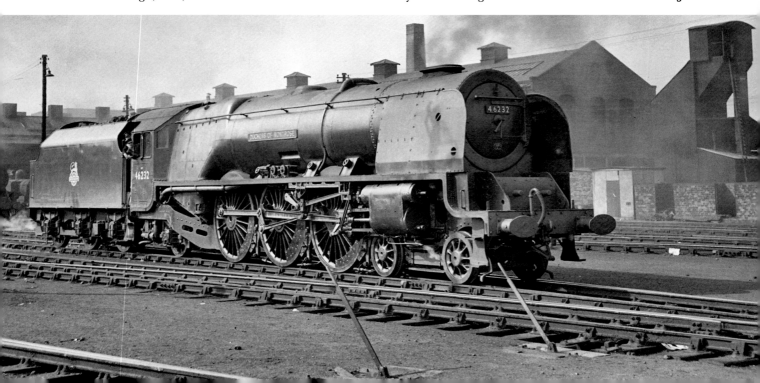

Polmadie's history with the Stanier 8F has been somewhat chequered, if brief. Whereas the WD 2-8-0 8F class were allocated in reasonable numbers – twenty-two in total – averaging a dozen or so between 1957 and 1962, the LMS 8Fs had basically two short periods of residency. The first occurred during World War Two when eight of the class were allocated at various times during the period from July 1943 to July 1944. Thereafter, and especially in BR days, they became quite rare in Scotland and only those engines visiting from the likes of Carlisle provided proof of their existence. However, in September 1957 three of the class were allocated to Polmadie. This trio though were not any old Stanier 8Fs because prior to them arriving at 66A they did not quite exist; at least in BR Book Stock. The three were all former War Department locomotives which BR had taken on for various reasons, all of which escape this compiler. They were originally LMS engines which had been seconded to the WD and were now basically demobbed. This is the first of them, No.48773 over the Polmadie ashpits in August 1962. None of the three were given their original LMS numbers and the numbers given by BR were created as though these were new locomotives: 48773, 48774, and 48775. Their short BR (Polmadie) history can be summarised as follows: 48773 (ex-WD 500) arrived 66A September 1957, withdrawn December 1962, re-instated January 1963, transferred to Kingmoor in October 1963, ended up in the north-west of England and survived until the end of steam on BR, being withdrawn in August 1968; 48774 (ex-WD 501) arrived 66A September 1957, withdrawn December 1962, re-instated January 1963, withdrawn June 1963, re-instated October 1963 and transferred to Kingmoor, withdrawn July 1965; 48775 (ex-WD 512) arrived 66A September 1957, withdrawn December 1962, re-instated January 1963, withdrawn June 1963, re-instated October 1963 and transferred to Kingmoor, like 48773 it too went to the NW of England and lasted until August 1968. One final thing of note which set this trio apart from the rest of the class was the large cover over the clack valves. *David J.Dippie.*

Involved in a recent side impact incident and suffering what might be described as 'heavy superficial damage', 'Clan' No.72001 CLAN CAMERON lay on Polmadie shed awaiting a report on 5th April 1961. It is recorded that this Pacific entered Cowlairs during the following June for a Heavy Intermediate overhaul which no doubt included repair to the damage shown here. It was the last major overhaul carried out on a Polmadie 'Clan' although a boiler change did not take place. Life for the 66A 'Clans' was precarious at any time but it is a wonder that 72001 survived even this 'minor' scrape! *David J.Dippie.*

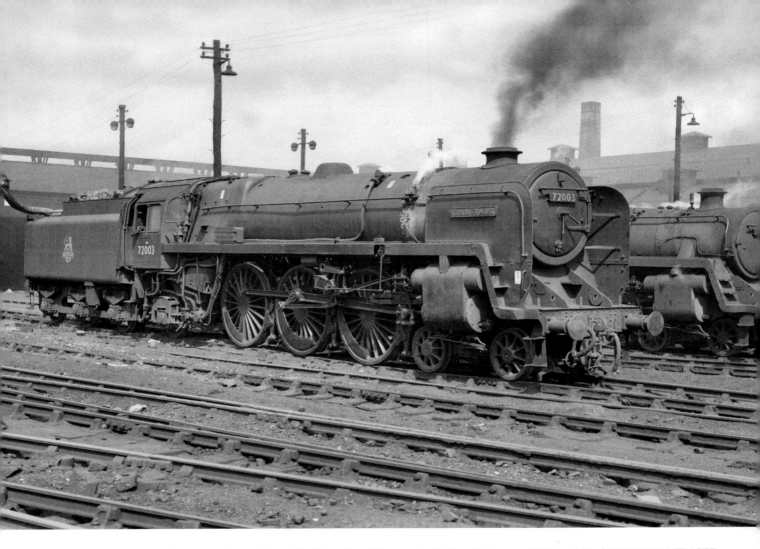

Another Polmadie 'Clan' but this one looks healthier, if a little dirty. The date is Friday 4th August 1961 and No.72003 CLAN FRASER takes on water whilst being prepared for what appears to be any evening job. Now, you might be forgiven in thinking that the date given for this illustration is incorrect but the date is exact because the original British Railways emblem worn by this locomotive was the same one it took to the scrapyard at Darlington two years later. It has been pointed out that No.72003 was the only BR Pacific, other than the ill-fated No.46202, which carried a BR emblem to its demise (*see also* No.41 in this series - *Darlington Scrapyard 1948-1964*). Why that happened is unclear especially since 72003 attended Cowlairs twice after the introduction of the BR crest in 1957 and ample opportunity arose at both subsequent dates. Anyway, no matter what kind of reception these Pacifics received at Polmadie, and elsewhere in Scotland, they still looked good recorded on film on a fine sunny day. *David J.Dippie.*

A double take!? One of the more popular 'Firth Brits' No.70052 FIRTH OF TAY copies the 'Clan' on that same afternoon in August 1961. No.72000 is behind. Happy days. *David J.Dippie.*

72000 CLAN BUCHANAN had been given a Heavy General overhaul in February 1961 (its final works visit) when it was also fitted with ATC/AWS. Here on the shed yard on 4th August 1961 it appears that cleaning was not a priority for this class, or indeed any other during a period when it became more difficult to recruit staff willing to climb the promotion ladder but starting at the bottom as an engine cleaner. Generally, Glasgow's other industries were paying better wages than BR at this time. Add that fact to the growing number of redundancies being suffered throughout the railway industry and suddenly a life on the railway was no longer regarded as a job for life. *David J.Dippie.*

It wasn't just the unpopular 'Clans' which appeared neglected by Polmadie in 1961. Just look at resident 'Duchess' No.46224 PRINCESS ALEXANDRA as she queues for the ash pit on that same August day. *David J.Dippie.*

CLAN CAMERON back in business on 21st April 1962. This was the last year for the Polmadie batch and it is amazing that their early demise did not raise too many eyebrows amongst the BR hierarchy; it certainly did amongst the world of enthusiasts. *David J. Dippie.*

(*above*) 72000 rides the 70ft articulated turntable at Polmadie in 1951 with plenty of room to spare. This turntable, located at the eastern end of the yard, was taken out and removed on Monday 4th November 1968, so bringing to an end any further steam related servicing activity at Polmadie. The new era had begun. (*below*) This is No.72004 CLAN MACDONALD in 1952, the same year that it was put into traffic. Unbelievable or what! *Both C.J.B.Sanderson.*

In total contrast and when things seemed rosier and steam was still king. No.72001, with bulled-up wheel rims and motion, after return from Crewe, takes water in 1953. *C.J.B.Sanderson.*

Obviously ex-works – especially being so clean at this late a date – BR Standard Class 5 No.73062 graces Polmadie yard on 3rd October 1959. Just four years old, the 4-6-0 was now firmly back at Polmadie after a stint at Motherwell earlier on in its career. No.73062 would now end its days here but some two years before the end of Scottish steam. Polmadie was well-off for these useful engines having an average of between ten and fifteen allocated from the 1954 and 1955 built batches. Their usual workings from Glasgow (Central) took them on expresses to Manchester (Victoria), Edinburgh (Waverley), and, during the summer season to Blackpool. Although our subject didn't, three of Polmadie's Std. 5s did survive until that fateful day in May 1967. A couple of things of interest appear in this illustration; firstly the new ATC/AWS acquired by 73062, and secondly, in the right background can be seen two of the ill-fated Metro-Vick Co-Bos which were off a Down *CONDOR* working and appear to be just as dirty as the steam locomotives at Polmadie. Ironically, these big, noisy, and unreliable diesels did not last much longer than the trio of 66A Standard 5s in question. *C.J.B.Sanderson.*

Having just topped off the tender tank, the crew of 'Royal Scot' No.46107 ARGYLL AND SUTHERLAND HIGHLANDER wait for the 'right away' to take their charge off shed on Saturday 21st April 1962. By now basically clapped-out, the Polmadie 'Scots' were running mainly secondary main line work including express freights although the expanding diesel fleet was to finally see them off by the end of the year. *David J.Dippie.*

As the Stanier Pacifics went into store or were withdrawn, it seemed a forgone conclusion that the big Type 4 diesels would completely rule the roost and nothing akin to the 'Duchesses' would be allocated ever again to Polmadie. How wrong we all were. Initially, shock was probably the biggest reaction to the events which unfolded in late 1963, quickly followed by questions. On 15th September 1963, three Thompson A2 Part 3 Pacifics, Nos.60512 STEADY AIM, 60522 STRAIGHT DEAL and 60524 HERRINGBONE were all sent to Polmadie. For nearly two years they resided, hardly working when compared with the ex-LMS Pacifics they apparently replaced. Numerous reasons were put forward for their presence at Polmadie and the most likely one given was 'to work out mileage' which, especially with hindsight, seems both lame and stupid or perhaps reasonable and stupid – they were funny times on BR the '60s. All three were painted with the diagonal yellow stripe on the cab sides which effectively banned them from working south of Crewe (some authorities on the LM Region thought they should be banned from working south of the Scottish border). Of course in reality they rarely worked south of Carlisle and, for long periods, they did nothing save the occasional substitution for a failed main line diesel. However, one recorded working saw No.60522 working over the S&C as far as Leeds. Finally No.60524 was condemned on 15th February 1965, and Nos.60512 and 60522 followed on 19th June. This is the first of that trio on 2nd May 1965 at the back of Polmadie shed, effectively 'out of the way' and biding its time prior to withdrawal. Note the concrete outline of a segment of the original 70ft diameter turntable pit just beyond the front of the A2. That table, a fairly young appliance, was repositioned at the eastern end of the yard in 1945. *N.W.Skinner.*

Arriving at Polmadie with the Thompson Pacifics were three Peppercorn A2s: Nos.60527 SUN CHARIOT, 60530 SAYAJIRAO, and 60535 HORNETS BEAUTY (the 66A lads, many of whom would be ex-Caley men, must have loved those names). This is the latter engine, again at the rear of the shed, on that second day of May 1965. Like the Thompson engines, these A2s were not to the liking of the Polmadie crews (a far cry from the reception given the A1s a dozen years before) and were reportedly stopped for the slightest niggle – shades of the 'Clans' on the old North British section? *N.W.Skinner.*

No.60527 was the first of the Peppercorn trio to be condemned, an event which took place on 24th April 1965, just before this illustration was captured on film. Meanwhile, No.60530 had left Polmadie on 31st July 1964, back to familiar territory and to where it was required at Dundee Tay Bridge shed. It fared better than the 66A lot and survived until condemned on 19th November 1966 but still ended up at the same scrap merchants in Motherwell. *N.W.Skinner.*

All three Pacifics in one vision! Stanier's nightmare or perhaps Thompson's dream!? A full house of ex-LNER motive power line-up in the back yard at Polmadie, 2nd May 1965. To make matters worse, there is a Gresley teak carriage on the left – at least the Master of LNER motive power got a look in, even if it was via his passenger stock. What was that ex-LNER carriage doing at 66A anyway? *N.W.Skinner.*

Yet another Peppercorn Pacific roams the rails of Polmadie. This one though has nothing to do with the others which were allocated at the time. No.60131 OSPREY is passing the coaling plant on Saturday 1st August 1964 in late afternoon. The reason why this Neville Hill A1 is in Glasgow brings much speculation to mind. It could have worked up the S&C; it could have worked a holiday extra from the likes of Scarborough (a favourite resort for Glaswegians), that board on the smokebox door indicates an excursion of sorts but it is not clear. It is clear that the tender requires topping up with coal and that is where the A1 is heading. The size of the coaling plant can be appreciated from this angle and from left to right the bunkers each held the following quantities of coal: 100 tons grade I; 200 tons of grade III; 100 tons grade II. However, by 1964 goodness knows what grade of coal was being dished out. Any answers to the A1s' presence would be appreciated. On a postcard.......... *C.J.B.Sanderson.*

En route to Central station on an August afternoon in 1962, 'Duchess' No.46250 CITY OF LICHFIELD and Fairburn Cl.4 No.42277 leave behind a momentous smokescreen for Polmadie shed and its neighbours; most of the action however appears to be coming from the Pacific, with the coupled 2-6-4T being dragged along as an unwilling partner. *David J.Dippie.*

The diesels have arrived! No, not any old diesels but the diesels. Settling down on shed road No.9, two Clayton Type 1 Bo-Bos, the nearest identified as D8519, are surrounded by their steam brethren. The date is 2nd August 1963 and soon these 900 h.p. centre-cab locomotives will create their own bit of history at Polmadie; in fact it had already started. However, unlike many of their forebears, it will be an inglorious history, but that is another story for another tome. The shed today is revealing an allocation which will basically take it to the end of steam in Scotland less than four years hence. There is not one 'namer' on show, certainly no Pacifics and, except for the diesels, all the engines are wearing a thick covering of filth. Note that the roof is now starting to show its age; a coincidence or another indication that maintenance was slipping in all aspects connected with steam motive power? *David J.Dippie.*

A view across the Polmadie ash pits on 8th May 1954 with a kind of hierarchy existing between the shunting tanks and goods engines on the left, through the mixed traffic ranks in the centre, and then finally, at the top of the tree, the passenger tenders engines. Simply put, the segregation started at the coaling plant where three bunkers fed three lines of engines. Nearer the main line was the bunker containing the top grade coal given exclusively to passenger engines whilst the centre bunker fed a third grade coal for shunting and goods types. The final bunker contained a second grade coal with the jigger feeder over that road was also connected to the second bunker to give a choice of coal for either mixed traffic locomotives or goods types. From the coaler the engines moved onto the ash pits usually keeping to the left, centre or right depending on their position when leaving the coaling plant. The ash plant was somewhat unique to the UK in that four 190ft long pits were built over two bunkers. The bottom of the pits, and the platform between each pair of tracks was constructed of old rails in such a way as to allow ash and clinker to fall through the resultant grate into the bunker below. Each bunker had a water trough where the ashes were immediately quenched. At the bottom of each trough was a continuous electrically driven conveyor belt able to shift the ash and clinker at a speed of 11ft per minute. These belts fed another wider belt which was located at the end of the pit belts and positioned at right angles. This belt discharged onto a further belt which was inclined and hoisted the ash aloft to a 50-ton capacity bunker positioned over a track where waiting wagons could be loaded by gravity. The whole ash plant scheme was constructed by the LMS and was completed shortly before BR came into being. *C.J.B.Sanderson.*

Three of the resident riffraff gather at the ash pits on Saturday 3rd October 1959. Graffiti – a very contradictory legend, 'Omo bright' – adorns the tender of 4F No.44193, coal covers the cab roof of ex-Caley 3F 0-6-0T No.56298, and WD 2-8-0 No.90549 lends support. When looking at all the express passenger engines, it is easy to forget that Polmadie shed also had a large allocation of locomotives which moved 44 **the goods, be it on the main or branch line, or in the yards. All were vital to the railway, and the country's well being.** *C.J.B.Sanderson.*

We could not leave out one of Stanier's finest, the Class 5 4-6-0. Possibly the best mixed traffic locomotive ever to run on British Railways, these locomotives appear to have had many short term relationships with Polmadie added to which only about ten were allocated at any one time. The longest serving engines managed about seven years apiece and only three managed that length of time. Some, again not many, put in five years or thereabouts. The majority were allocated from a couple of months up to about three years which was surprising really, considering the loyalty shown by many other classes. No.45459 was a case in point; arriving at 66A in October 1958, it was gone by March 1960. Here in 1959 it is seen passing the depot's primary water tank and the ash hopper provided by the LMS in the late 1940s. *C.J.B.Sanderson.* 45

Former Caledonian Railway 2F 0-6-0 No.57321 stables in the sunshine at Polmadie on Saturday 5th June 1954. More than thirty of these useful and dependable locomotives were allocated to 66A during the BR period up to 1960, a number little changed since the days when the LMS first took over in 1923! *C.J.B.Sanderson.*

It wasn't all glamour. In fact none of it was. On Saturday 6th May 1961, Kingmoor's Hughes/Fowler 'Crab' No.42882 – apparently – takes a weekend break from its mundane duties and is amongst friends and fellow 'strugglers' the WD 2-8-0s. A low fire is keeping the locomotive warm and ready for work and a return home on Monday morning. Though regular visitors to Polmadie from the likes of Kingmoor, Hamilton, etc., the class was rather shy when it came to residing at 66A. In BR days only Nos.42738 (9/59–3/62), and 42850 (9/59–7/62 withdrawal) managed to put some time in whereas in pre-war days five of the class spent much of the '30s at Polmadie and only moved on at the outbreak of the war. No.42882 appears ready for the scrapyard but it was still putting in some excellent performances despite its atrocious external condition. All things must pass though and the 2-6-0 was eventually condemned during that mass cull of December 1962. *C.J.B.Sanderson.*

Polmadie certainly was cosmopolitan in the variety of classes allocated and the visitors added to that mix. Many of the BR Standard types were represented at 66A but the Cl.4 2-6-0s were latecomers to the shed, none being allocated until 1964 at the earliest. Prior to that however members of the class were regular visitors and Motherwell's No.76000 is seen on the shed yard in 1953 surrounded by a mix of locomotives representing a much earlier generation. Polmadie's first batch arrived in December 1964 in the shape of Nos.76004, 76070 and 76071. They were later supplemented in early 1966 by Nos.76103, 76104, 76105 but one of those was withdrawn on arrival. Only No.76104 stuck it out to the end in May '67. The odd-shaped tower structure in the right background was the depot's sand kiln, also provided by the LMS. *David J.Dippie.*

Former Caley 2P 0-4-4T No.55228 was one of only a dozen of her kind to be found at Polmadie in 1950 when this photograph was taken. By the end of the decade the situation had remained the same but the engines themselves had been shuffled around so that only about half of the 1950 engines were still at 66A in 1959. Our subject here was one of those which stayed put. Strangely enough, the latter BR period was little changed from 1935 when a similar number of these handy four-coupled tanks were resident; amongst them of course was No.15228 – to give it the LMS identification of the period. *C.J.B.Sanderson.*

WD 2-8-0 No.90134 looks considerably clean compared to most of the class. The reason why is simple to understand because the 2-8-0 had recently undergone a Heavy General overhaul at Cowlairs (11th February to 20th March 1954) and was living off the paint job for now. The date is 8th May 1954 so just over six weeks have elapsed since it was put back into traffic. Allocated to Polmadie from 23rd February 1952 to 16th October 1961, it was a useful engine which, though seemingly disliked, was regarded by footplatemen as more than able to do its job. The WD has just filled its tender with some choice coal (the track it is on indicates that it has just left the bunker 'serving' lower grade coal 'for goods engines and shunting types'). Behind is the conveyor belt which lifted ash and clinker from the underground collectors into a larger bunker served by waiting empty wagons – on the right – which would be taken away to a suitable tip. Interestingly, the road on which the WD stands, and the next one towards the cameraman, have been strengthened by fixing two lengths of bull-head rail to the sleepers on each side of the running rails for a distance equal to the dimensions of the locomotive wheelbase. Perhaps some subsidence issues had cropped up? *C.J.B.Sanderson.*

CORKERHILL

A busy yard scene at Corkerhill on 18th May 1959 with ex-LMS types dominating the stabling roads, although the BR Standards are also presenting a show. This is the west end of the shed with various landmarks just visible. On the left, just above the 2P, is the lifting shop, a British Railways-built structure which was erected over the existing hoist. Just right of centre can be seen the square profile of the LMS-built No.1 size coaling plant. The roof of the shed, at this end of the building, is now in a style first introduced by the LMS and later perpetuated by BR to eliminate the original northlight roof which was showing its 1896 origins as only the northlight roofs could, with a rapid deterioration of the timbers once the rot had started. Corkerhill was the largest of the former Glasgow & South Western engine sheds with an allocation averaging ninety to a hundred locomotives for much of its latter existence. By May 1959 BR Standards, which accounted for about a third of the allocation, had ousted many of the pre-Grouping survivors although nearly a dozen of the 'old-timers' clung on. The LMS 2P 4-4-0s could also muster a dozen of their ilk too although their larger 4P cousins, the compounds had all gone. The Standards, accompanied by a handful of Stanier Class 5s, were to be the mainstay of the steam allocation until closure of the shed in the early summer of 1967. Identifiable here are 40597 (from Hurlford), and residents 73121 and 45194. Nowadays Corkerhill depot is still functioning, albeit in a much rebuilt form, and deals mainly with multiple units (what else is there?) of both electric and diesel types. Today the atmosphere above the shed is nothing like as bad as depicted in this illustration (although that is not too bad and was at least an indicator of the location of the shed for the spotting' fraternity newcomers arriving on foot!) however many of the polluting and poison elements of the modern combustion engine cannot be seen! *N.W.Skinner.*

51

Two members of the 1950 allocation wearing the pre-dominant coating of grime and two sizes of the BRITISH RAILWAYS tender insignia. (*top*) 3F 0-6-0 No.57698 was one of twenty pre-Group six-coupled goods engines which took care of the diminishing goods traffic handled by Corkerhill's engines. Note the perforated cab side sheet which once had a tablet-catcher fitted in a previous life north of this location. Behind the tender can be seen the engine hoist which was to be cocooned inside its own building before the decade was out. (*below*) Since their introduction to the G&SW lines by the LMS, Corkerhill had maintained an allocation of nine of these 4P Compounds which could be found working to Carlisle or to any of the coastal destinations served by St Enoch's passenger services. No.40919 had been loyal to 67A (27J as it was then) since before 1935 but by February 1954 the BR Standards had muscled in and the scrapyard at Kilmarnock locomotive works beckoned. The 3F was less fortunate. Transferring to Hurlford in January 1951, the six-coupled goods was condemned a year later (the ex-Highland Railway engine had perhaps ventured too far south). *Both C.J.B.Sanderson.*

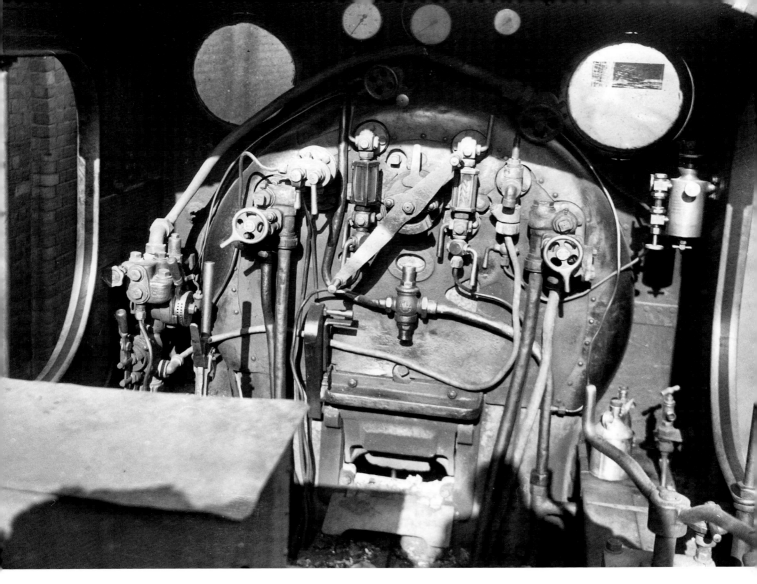

One for the modellers'! This nice bright backplate view of ex-Caley McIntosh 1899 3F No.57596 was captured at Corkerhill in 1950 when the 0-6-0 was out of traffic, probably stopped for repairs. Note that the engine is square-on to the early morning sunlight with the shadows of the cab hand rails creating the illusion of an attractive inlaid – brass-steel-brass – metal finish to the cut-out cover strips. *C.J.B.Sanderson.*

(*above*) A nice broadside of 'Jubilee' No.45560 PRINCE EDWARD ISLAND with the original northlight roof (in actuality a westernlight roof) shed forming the backdrop. The date is sometime in 1950 and the 4-6-0 is still wearing the unlined red livery with no British Railways recognition whatsoever except the addition of 40000 to its number; 5XP still adorns the cabside, below the correct Gill sans figures. Acquired from Kingmoor in 1942, this engine returned to England ten years later but went to Nottingham as part of a swap deal (*see later*) with the London Midland Region. Mention earlier of the terrible state of the shed roof at this time is borne out in this illustration. Eventually all six roads at this end of the building were re-roofed but the fitting shop at the extreme left (with the smallest roof ventilator) kept its northlight section intact. *C.J.B.Sanderson.*

(*opposite*) It is well-known that the BR 'Clan' Pacifics were not the most popular engines in Scotland; Polmadie's batch were tried everywhere. Those allocated to Kingmoor had a somewhat better reception and managed a longer existence by three or more years in certain cases although some of those were sent to 'exotic' areas of the system for trials which came to nothing; our subject here for instance spent a few months on former Great Eastern metals in late 1958, working out of Stratford shed. No.72009 CLAN STEWART, seen at Corkerhill on 17th May 1964, came from the English camp and had well over twelve months operational life ahead of it on this Sunday, whereas the five Polmadie engines had long since been reduced to scrap. However, all is not what it seems here. Although in steam, the cylinder end plates on both cylinders had been taken off – one was on the front footplate whilst the other is on the ground below the cylinder. Whatever was being done to the cylinders is unknown but it provided overtime for somebody; securing those fixing nuts alone would have taken an hour for each side, as for the work therein? *A.Ives.*

With the aid of the vacuum tractor, Standard Class 4 No.76090 was turned effortlessly by the Corkerhill turntable on 28th July 1957. Not long since 'out of the box' the 2-6-0 has certainly built up a nice coating of filth since its arrival at 67A just weeks beforehand. Out of the eventual Scottish Region allocation of these engines, Corkerhill would have ten on its books by the following spring. *C.J.B.Sanderson.*

Now then! What about this? A rather immaculate LMS-built McIntosh 0-4-4T No.55266 struts around the shed yard at Corkerhill in 1953. This was not an example of a recently ex-St Rollox works engine but was one of those locomotives looked after by the shed, and probably a particular crew, for performing a specific high profile, or in the public gaze, type of job. The paintwork has a patina about it which stems from months if not years of cleaning and polishing. There is a reference to 2.50 painted on the footplate skirting just behind the buffer – the last shopping date? – with an unknown symbol to the left of the figures. The bufferbeam carries a certain amount of ingrained dirt which was probably attained by the application of a paraffin rag to keep it clean; no new paint there. The painted embellishments are clearly for show. Note the extension bar on the smokebox door securing wheel; now that would make for easier access to the box. Corkerhill had ten of these ex-Caley tanks allocated during the early BR period but by 1953 some of the 1895-built engines had been called to the scrapyard. No.55266 was the final version of this type and the ten members of the batch each weighed in at just below 60-tons. *C.J.B.Sanderson.*

How the mighty..... No.55266 on 18th May 1959. No longer the 'show-off', and certainly not looking its best. By now the front numberplate has been located higher on the smokebox door whilst the shedplate has found its proper place, at the bottom. Although prepared for long-term storage; this illustration could show it at the end of winter storage awaiting a call back to traffic. Withdrawal was still two years away, in September 1961, after which the one-time pride of 67A would be sold for scrap. *N.W.Skinner.*

This ancient and somewhat battered former Highland Railway Travelling Post Office stood as part of the breakdown train at Corkerhill shed in 1950. Branded as LMS Tool Van No.354398 (LMS Service stock), the vehicle started life as a bogie version of the HR Type C, to Diagram 41, of which it is known three existed. The legend 6.8.34 painted on the solebar, with a further legend K77 painted beneath, may well have been the last paint/overhaul dates. The proximity of Kilmarnock leads one to assume that the 'K' has some connection with that works although Barassie would surely have been involved. The curious roof ventilators/toplights are worthy of note but nothing more, except perhaps derogatory comment! However, this type of roof was, it appears, normal for the TPO designs on the HR and possibly Scotland too as some ex-G&SWR TPOs were similarly 'covered'. Does anyone know of its fate under BR? *C.J.B.Sanderson.*

Stopped for repairs on Sunday 2nd May 1965, Standard Cl.2 No.78026 was a relative newcomer to the Corkerhill allocation having been transferred from the outpost at Stranraer during the previous November. It was the first and only one of its kind to work from 67A and was given a rather 'cushy' job working as St Enoch pilot until that terminus closed in June 1966. To months later, with increasing dieselisation and lack of suitable work to perform, No.78026 was withdrawn having made its mark on Corkerhill's history. Stanier Cl.5 No.44798 represented a class which was anything but a rarity at this place although it too was relatively new, in allocation terms, having transferred from Inverness in June 1960. It was just of LMS parentage having been sent new to the former Highland headquarters in October 1947. In terms of longevity, No.44798 was withdrawn immediately after the Cl.2 so just missed out on its twentieth birthday. The pair were peeping out of the southernmost roads at the west end of the shed; a building which can only be described as 'adequate for purpose!' *N.W.Skinner.*

The disposal of a steam locomotive was and still is one of the dirtiest jobs going, coupled to the fact that it is also difficult for various reasons – ask any volunteer at a preserved railway centre. In June 1954 it was just the same as it is now except that there were more locomotives to dispose of and, it was endless; a real 24/7 job! Former Caley 2F 0-6-0 No.57266 was being taken through the procedure at its home shed on Saturday 5th June 1954. Somebody inside the cab was cleaning the fire, with the fruits of their labours filling the narrow gauge tub alongside. The exact amount of ash and clinker a motive power depot like Corkerhill used to generate must have been enormous and was yet another headache for the powers-that-be to worry about. No wonder diesel and electric locomotion became the much needed revolution. *C.J.B.Sanderson.*

The new order at the ashpits, in June 1954! BR Standard Cl.4 2-6-4T No.80009 makes a splash from its full side tank as the disposal men move the rather smart engine onto the ash pit. Already eighteen months old, the Cl.4 looks as if it has just arrived from works but that is definitely not the case. Like 2P No.55266 featured earlier, this engine appears to have been adopted by a particular crew who have not only 'bulled up' the tank with elbow grease but have also added subtle touches of paint to the front end. Perhaps the same crew which cherished the 0-4-4T had been given this Standard as their new charge and so discarded their old one? Nevertheless, 80009 in June 1954 was a credit to its crew; such could not be said during the following decade. This particular Cl.4 was the last of a batch of ten built for the Scottish Region of which three went new to Corkerhill at the end of 1952 and the beginning of 1953. Of course many more followed but others had preceded them too: 80024 to 80026 in December 1951 – it seems that 67A was receiving Christmas gifts regularly – 80046 and 80047 in September and October 1952, 80051 and 80053 in December 1952! Others came and went but a hard core remained loyal to 67A throughout: 80008, 80009, 80024, 80025, and 80127. They were popular engines at Corkerhill and created some creditable annual mileages between them. It also fell to this class to be the last operational steam locomotives at 67A when Scottish Region banished steam in May 1967. *C.J.B.Sanderson.*

A quiet moment around the Corkerhill ash plant in September 1965, with Cl.5 No.44882 located over the pits. Business is no longer brisk in this section of the yard and within a couple of years this plant will be redundant, a dinosaur of the steam age, albeit a fairly late addition to the great scheme of things. Note that the clinker tubs are already being dumped as soon as a problem arises with any of them. The '5' was part of the Barrow allocation at this time and had been to Cowlairs works for repairs during the summer. However, this engine was no stranger to Corkerhill having spent much of its life allocated to Kingmoor. It was to return to the Carlisle depot prior to withdrawal which took place shortly after steam was banished from the Scottish Region. *F.Coulton.*

Loyal to the end No.80127 stables alongside the water column at the west end. The date is 17th May 1964, more than three years away from the end of steam on the Scottish Region. The Cl.4 tank was not yet ten years old but it was certainly looking traffic weary and would not get any better than this externally. To the right is a couple of the diesel shunters of the next generation which, it might be added, would serve BR for much longer than any of the Standards did. Horwich-built D3923, which was equally as dirty as 80127, was one of a batch of five 0-6-0DE shunters acquired new by 67A in January and February 1961; they were all still going strong thirty years later. Although well equipped with ash pits and all the associated machinery that went with that disposal sequence, it will be noted that, unlike most engine shed yards on British Railways, Corkerhill was bereft of outside pits. That applied to both ends of the shed and must have made life a tad more difficult for the enginemen lubricating their charges, and the fitters adjusting that last minute 'turn' which could pass or fail a locomotive into traffic. *A.Ives.*

In September 1952 the majority of the 'Jubilees' allocated to Corkerhill shed were transferred, en masse, to depots in England and in return, an equal number of England based 'Jubilees' were drafted off to Corkerhill. One of those affected was No.45621 NORTHERN RHODESIA which came from Millhouses; others included 45665, 45687, 45711, and 45720. No.45693 AGAMEMNON, which had transferred to Corkerhill in January 1944 from Kingmoor, was unaffected by the mass swap and continued working from 67A until withdrawn in December 1962. Of course there were more engines affected than those listed for Corkerhill, Polmadie too was involved. Our subject was photographed at Corkerhill in June 1954, shortly after a visit to the works at St Rollox it would appear, because the cab side figures are those applied only at the Glasgow establishment. *C.J.B.Sanderson.*

An undated photograph of Gresley A3 No.60038 FIRDAUSSI standing at the east end of Corkerhill shed shortly after running over from St Enoch station at the conclusion of its working into Glasgow with the Down *THAMES-CLYDE EXPRESS*. One of eight based at Holbeck shed, this Pacific was the longest serving at 55A – February 1960 to June 1963 – and was a regular visitor to Corkerhill, along with its compatriots, until the diesel-electrics took over the Anglo-Scottish express workings. The building on the right was the new administration and amenities block – a sign over the main doorway gave the name as Muster Hall – which was a great improvement on the cramped accommodation incorporated into the shed. *David J.Dippie.*

As mentioned previously, Stanier 8Fs were not all that common in Scotland during BR days, so this view of Kingmoor's No.48756 at Corkerhill on 24th September 1961 is a treat for one and all. *I.W.Coulson.*

At one time, indeed up to about 1964, it would have been a rare event to find a mixed traffic tender engine from an English shed other than perhaps Carlisle or Leeds. However, from about that time Cowlairs works started to take in Stanier Class 5s from a number of sheds in north-west England. This is Trafford Park's No.45404 which has been given the Cowlairs treatment at the front end, including the obligatory painting on the bufferbeam of the name of the locomotive's home shed. Though undated, the photograph was probably taken circa September 1965 when Cowlairs released the '5' for running-in after it had been on works for a number of months. Looking at the tender, perhaps that was the reason for the somewhat elongated visit – awaiting a 'new' tender. That particular tender appears as though it has not been following the same route as the engine for some time so had come from another. Is it green, because photographic evidence reveals that quite a few Class 5s ended up with green tenders during those latter years of BR steam; also note the axlebox covers which are the Timken roller bearing type which were not altogether common with the Class 5 tenders except some of the latter built engines put into traffic on either side of Nationalisation. This view also reveals the lightweight corrugated cladding which covered all six roads of the shed at this time; it looked draughty but at least the shed was well ventilated. *F.Coulton.*

A rather cloudy 6th August 1963 reveals a typical Corkerhill shed scene of the period with BR Standards Nos.73121 and 80005, Stanier Class 5s Nos.44706 and 44791, an unidentified 'Peak' diesel locomotive and a Cravens-built multiple unit sharing the yard. The number of brick arch components and brake blocks is quite noticeable and leaves one wondering what happened to all those steam locomotive related 'consumables' when BR eventually 'pulled the plug' in 1968; remember this is just one depot so the total amount must have run into hundreds, if not thousands, of tons. The big diesel would have arrived in Glasgow after bringing one of the St Pancras-St Enoch expresses via the G&SW route. They took over from the Gresley A3s whose short reign on the workings was noticeable for its brevity. *David J. Dippie.*

(*above*) 'Royal Scot' No.46102, formerly named BLACK WATCH, lies dead and forlorn at Corkerhill on 6th August 1963. Nameplate, badge and shed plate missing, the 7P has been unceremoniously dumped after its withdrawal at the end of the previous December. The 'Scot' arrived at Corkerhill on transfer from Polmadie in October 1962. *David J.Dippie.* (*below*) One of 67A's own Jubilee's, No.45687, minus NEPTUNE nameplates, stands forlorn at Corkerhill on 1st March 1963 looking for all intents and purposes as though it was in store. However, like the 7P it too had been withdrawn in the previous December. No.45692, ex-CYCLOPS, was in the same predicament. *C.J.B.Sanderson.*

In the same line-up as No.46102 at 67A on that August day in 1963, was this little gathering consisting of ex-LMS 2P No.40615, ex-Caley 2P Nos.55221 and 55203 (the former undertook stationary boiler duties as its last job, and had lost a set of coupled wheels in the process, before being condemned), along with an unidentified 'Scot'. This scrap line was in a continuous state of flux. As one engine was hauled away to the breakers, another would take its place. Through some unknown force, or perfectly logical reason, it was possible for certain engines to remain in these dumps at depots for some years whilst others lingered for a matter of weeks or even days before succumbing to the call of the scrapyard. Of the trio illustrated, which were all withdrawn in 1961 at Corkerhill, the 2P was finished during October 1961 whereas 55221 was withdrawn in September and may have then been pressed into SB duties because it apparently didn't join this line-up until after 1st March 1963 (information regarding that situation would be welcome). No.55203 had been withdrawn in the December. Considering that these hulks had been here for such a time, two of them still have works plates adorning their bodyside, as well as front numberplates. Corkerhill also maintained another dump for its engines some miles away at Lugton and at that place a number of 67A 'Jubilees' – Nos.45621, 45665, 45707, 45711 and 45720, had the company of 2P 4-4-0s and even a 'Duchess' Pacific. Behind this sorry bunch stands the former coaling stage which was still in use as a water tank but its timber cladding had long since disappeared; the substantial girders were still doing a good job after sixty-odd years. *David J.Dippie.*

Considering that this Corkerhill based 'Scot' had also been withdrawn in December 1962, it begs the question as to why it was in steam on 1st March 1963? Did a motive power shortage see it temporarily re-activated? It was not unusual for withdrawn motive power to be put back into traffic, especially during the period under review, in order to meet traffic demands. Remember that Corkerhill's two 'Scots' arrived in October '62 and were withdrawn at the end of the year in favour of diesel traction taking on the main line passenger work. But those with memories of that particular winter will remember the carnage wrought upon the diesels as the cold played havoc with coolant systems and batteries. Note also that No.46104 SCOTTISH BORDERER is carrying nameplates and that the front end of the engine is quite presentable - for the period, remarkably so. Standard Class 4 No.80021 (in the 'normal' attire of filth) is coupled up behind. The pair are located alongside the residential housing which was created and built by the Glasgow & South Western Railway for their employees working within the new village of Corkerhill in 1896, long before the suburbs of Glasgow expanded out from the centre of the city and engulfed the area. *C.J.B.Sanderson.*